D1712540

# Writers Who Changed the World

# CHARLES DICKENS

Anita Croy

LUCENT PRESS

Description: New York : Lucent Press, 2020. | Series: Writers who changed the world | Includes glossary and index.
Identifiers: ISBN 9781534565876 (pbk.) | ISBN 9781534565883 (library bound) | ISBN 9781534565890 (ebook)
Subjects: LCSH: Dickens, Charles, 1812-1870--Juvenile literature. | Novelists, English--19th century--Biography--Juvenile literature.
Classification: LCC PR4581.C79 2020 | DDC 823.8 B--dc23

Printed in the United States of America

CPSIA compliance information: Batch #BS19KL: For further information contact Greenhaven Publishing LLC, New York, New York at 1-844-317-7404.

Please visit our website, www.greenhavenpublishing.com. For a free color catalog of all our high-quality books, call toll free 1-844-317-7404 or fax 1-844-317-7405.

# CONTENTS

# CHAPTER 1

This is a portrait of
Charles Dickens in the 1860s.

# CHARLES DICKENS
## Biography

**Born:** February 7, 1812

**Place of birth:** Portsmouth, England

**Mother:** Elizabeth Culliford Dickens

**Father:** John Dickens

**Famous for:** Writing some of the most loved books in English literature including *Oliver Twist*, *A Christmas Carol* (novella), and *Great Expectations*.

**How he changed the world:**
The social commentary in Charles Dickens's novels exposed some of the worst problems of Great Britain's industrialized society. Dickens helped persuade the government to take action against some of those problems.

*The* works of Charles Dickens DREW ATTENTION to the SOCIAL INJUSTICE of the nineteenth century and gave a VOICE to the POOR.

# LONDON CHILDHOOD

Charles Dickens is closely associated with London, the capital of England, which is the setting for many of his novels. However, he spent his early life in Chatham, a small naval town on the Thames River in Kent. The family was wealthy enough to employ a maid and send Charles to school. He loved reading and even wrote his own stories, such as "Misnar, Sultan of India."

In 1822, when Dickens was 10 years old, his family moved to London. His father worked in the Navy Pay Office, but he spent more money than he earned and the family got into debt. In London, the family lived in just two rooms and Charles slept in a closet.

*In 1824, Dickens's father was sent to a debtors' prison.*

Charles had to give up going to school. Instead, he got a job in a factory making black shoe polish to raise money for the family. He hated it. He worked 10 hours a day, 6 days a week, but his small salary was not enough to pay off his father's debts. In 1824, his father was sent to a debtors' prison with the rest of the Dickens family except Charles and his older sister, Fanny. The rest of the family stayed in prison until Charles's father was able to pay his debts.

## Words that changed the world

*In Bleak House, Dickens wrote,"As much mud in the streets as if the waters had but newly retired from the face of the earth … Smoke lowering down from chimney-pots, making a soft black drizzle, with flakes of soot in it as big as full-grown snow … Dogs, undistinguishable in mire. Horses, scarcely better; splashed to their very blinkers. Foot passengers, jostling one another's umbrellas in a general infection of ill-temper, and losing their foothold at street-corners, where tens of thousands of other foot passengers have been slipping and sliding since the day broke…"*

This British postage stamp shows the River Thames in London, with St. Paul's Cathedral in the background.

## Exploring the text

This excerpt from *Bleak House* (1852) gives a glimpse of what life is like in London in winter in the middle of the 1800s. Dickens begins by comparing the mud to Noah's flood in the Bible, and describes how it coats dogs and horses in the streets. The rapid increase in the city's population to around 1.3 million and the growing number of factories meant London's air was thick with smog from burning coal fires. The unpaved streets were churned into mud by the constant motion of people and animals.

## HISTORY'S STORY

Working in the shoe polish factory was a humiliating experience for the young Charles Dickens. His job was to seal and label the jars. He worked in the factory window, where passersby stopped to watch him work. He never forgot the embarrassment of having to do such a menial task.

# NOVELIST
# OF LONDON

Two years after leaving the debtors' prison, John Dickens again got into debt. Charles had gone back to school for a while, but his father could no longer afford to pay for his schooling. In May 1827, at age 15, Dickens got a job as a clerk in a law firm. On his first day at work, he was beaten up in the street. When Dickens told his bosses, they were amazed by his lively storytelling. Dickens worked at the firm for two years. He entertained his colleagues with his stories and his remarkable knowledge of London.

After leaving the law firm, Dickens went to work as a court reporter. His job was to write newspaper reports about the legal cases he heard. The courts were an ideal place to observe human behavior and hear all kinds of stories. Dickens next took a job as a political reporter, reporting on the British parliament. As well as writing about debates, Dickens began writing his own stories.

As a reporter in the Houses of Parliament, Dickens got to see how politicians made new laws.

## First success

In 1833, Charles wrote "Dinner at Poplar Walk," a funny story about two cousins eating together. He took it to the office of the *Monthly Magazine*. The magazine published the story and asked for more. Dickens wrote more stories, which he signed using the nickname of his youngest brother, "Boz." Soon, he decided to write a longer story about a group of friends who form a club named the Pickwick Club.

The Pickwick Papers was Dickens's first big hit. The first installment appeared in March 1836. A new chapter was published every month until the book was complete. The story was an

*The Pickwick Papers* told of the antics of Mr. Pickwick and his friends in a long series of separate episodes.

immediate hit. Readers waited impatiently each month for the next chapter. The public loved Dickens's different characters, particularly the servant Sam Weller. Dickens had a gift for capturing the different ways in which people speak. He made Weller's words sound like the Cockney accents he heard on London's streets. After the last chapter was published in 1837, the story was also published as a single book.

## HISTORY'S STORY

Publishing a novel in installments was common in the 1800s. Most people could not afford books, so they bought magazines that published novels chapter by chapter. While he was writing *The Pickwick Papers*, Dickens also began writing *Oliver Twist* for another magazine. To keep his readers interested, Dickens learned to end each installment with a cliffhanger.

# VICTORIAN SUPERSTAR

*The Pickwick Papers* made "Boz"
famous—and people soon figured
out that Boz was Charles Dickens. By
the time the novel was published as a
book in 1837, Dickens had married his
wife, Catherine Hogarth, and started
a family. He bought a nice house in
London. He also signed a contract
for his second novel, *Oliver Twist*.
The two stories were very different.
*The Pickwick Papers* was a comedy, but
life for the orphan Oliver was tough.
The first installment of *Oliver Twist*
appeared in February 1837.

This statue shows Dickens
with Little Nell, heroine of
*The Old Curiosity Shop*.

Dickens worked constantly. As well as
writing new chapters for his novels, he
continued to write for *Monthly Magazine* and he became the editor of a
newspaper, *Bentley's Miscellany*. As editor, he got to publish other writers'
stories. He enjoyed being able to help other writers.

Life was good, but tragedy was not far away. Dickens was friendly with
his sister-in-law, Mary, who lived with the family. Mary died suddenly in
May 1837. Dickens was so upset he missed his deadlines for the latest
chapters of both his novels. It was the only time he ever missed a deadline.

## More best sellers

Dickens published more novels in serial form. He began
*Nicholas Nickleby* in March 1838, publishing a chapter each month
for the next 20 months. For his next novels, *The Old Curiosity Shop*
and *Barnaby Rudge*, he decided to publish a new chapter each week.

The novels were huge hits, and Dickens's popularity spread
beyond England. *The Old Curiosity Shop* was a best seller in the
United States, where readers were desperate to know the latest
plot twists. Dickens left the heroine Little Nell dangerously
sick at the end of one installment of the
novel. When ships arrived in the United
States carrying the next chapter, crowds
of readers gathered at the docks to find
out what became of her.

## Crossing the Atlantic Ocean

Dickens decided the time was right
to visit the United States. He planned
a tour of readings in different cities.
Dickens already had a reputation as a
popular performer in London. Audiences
enjoyed listening to him reading out
extracts from his novels with dramatic
actions and different accents.

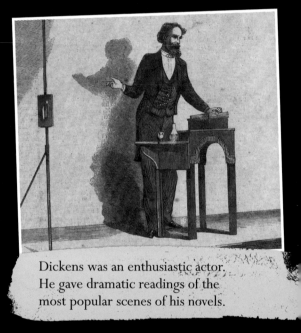

Dickens was an enthusiastic actor.
He gave dramatic readings of the
most popular scenes of his novels.

With Catherine, he set sail for the United States on January 2,
1842. The visit was not the triumph Dickens had hoped for. Always
worried about money, he was irritated to learn that American
publishers had published his books without paying him. He did
not enjoy reading criticism about himself in the newspapers.
But the public loved him, and large crowds turned up to his
performances. He returned to England almost six months later.

# CHAPTER 2

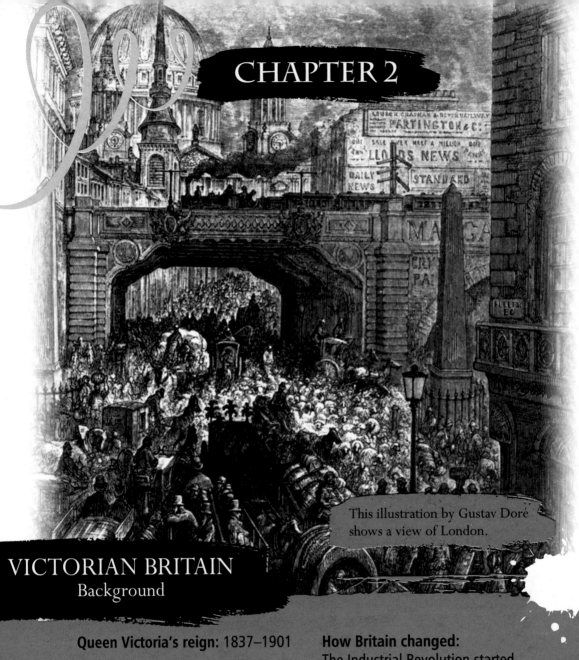

This illustration by Gustav Doré shows a view of London.

# VICTORIAN BRITAIN
## Background

**Queen Victoria's reign:** 1837–1901

**Population in 1801:** 16 million

**Population in 1901:** More than 40 million

**What happened:** During Victoria's reign, Great Britain became the world's most powerful and wealthy nation.

**How Britain changed:** The Industrial Revolution started in Great Britain in the late 1700s. Steam power and machines replaced the horse and human labor. This allowed goods to be made in large numbers.

*Huge* CHANGE was taking place in Britain during the TIME of Dickens's novels. INDUSTRIALIZATION was changing the FACE not only of the British LANDSCAPE, but also its SOCIETY. Dickens DOCUMENTED all these CHANGES in his NOVELS.

# INDUSTRIAL BRITAIN

Charles Dickens lived during a period of great change. Great Britain was the center of the Industrial Revolution, which had begun in the late 1700s. The invention of steam engines led to the appearance of new factories and mills full of machines that operated all day and night. Workers were needed to operate these machines, and hundreds of thousands of people moved to the cities that grew rapidly around the factories. They hoped to find steady work and better pay.

*Charles Dickens lived during a period of great change.*

The new cities were filthy from all the coal burned to power the steam engines. Living conditions were overcrowded and unhealthy. Many factory jobs were boring and dirty. They were also dangerous because of the moving machines. Children as young as 10 years old worked in factories or in coal mines. Many people failed to earn a good living. They joined a growing class of desperately poor people living in areas that were like slums.

At the same time, some parts of life improved. Prices tumbled as goods became cheaper to produce. The world's first passenger railroad opened between the northern cities of Liverpool and Manchester in 1830. It was an immediate success. Soon railroads were being built across the country. They made it easier for people to move around for work or for pleasure.

## Words that changed the world

*In* Hard Times, *Dickens wrote, "Coketown ... was a town of unnatural red and black like the painted face of a savage. It was a town of machinery and tall chimneys, out of which interminable serpents of smoke trailed themselves for ever ... It had a black canal in it, and a river that ran purple with ill-smelling dye, and vast piles of building full of windows where there was a rattling and a trembling all day long, and where the piston of the steam-engine worked monotonously up and down, like the head of an elephant in a state of melancholy madness."*

## Exploring the text

Dickens published *Hard Times* in 1854. He set the novel in "Coketown," a fictional town based on industrial cities in northern England, such as Manchester. His description of Coketown suggests that the factories were destroying everything around them and ruining the lives of the workers who spent their time inside. He likens the rising and falling piston of a steam engine to the nodding of a sad, crazy elephant. The novel describes the gulf between the rich factory owners and the poor workers.

In industrial towns, the air was full of smoke from the fires used to heat steam engines.

## HISTORY'S STORY

Dickens's novels show how industrialization has caused many problems. He describes how most people live in poverty. Dickens does show how some people grew richer, but he was more interested in the lives of the poor than those of the middle classes.

# PLIGHT OF
# THE POOR

In the middle of the 1800s, most people were poor. Wages were still low, and rent and other costs were high. There was no time off. If someone got sick and did not work, they did not get paid. To try to make enough money to survive, every member of a family often went out to work. Some children began working so young that they never went to school. Many others left school early.

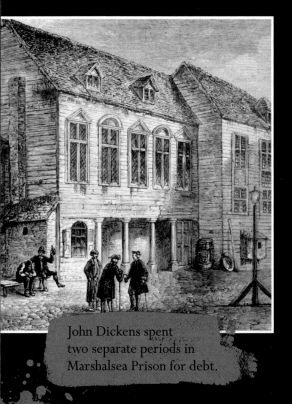

John Dickens spent two separate periods in Marshalsea Prison for debt.

There was no government help for the poor and sick. People were expected to look after themselves. Being in debt was seen as a crime. Dickens's father, John, was sent to Marshalsea Prison on the bank of the River Thames in London in 1824 for being in debt. In such cases, the whole family was usually imprisoned. If the family had any money, it could pay to stay in one of the prison's better rooms. It could also buy a pass to leave prison in order to earn money to pay off their debts. The poorest prisoners lived in the worst rooms. Many starved to death because they could not afford to buy food.

## Life in the workhouse

People who were too poor to have anywhere to live moved to the workhouse. The Poor Law of 1815 made each parish, or district, responsible for looking after its poor residents. Some parishes set up workhouses. These were places where, in exchange for doing work such as breaking up stones to use in construction or unpicking old ropes so they could be reused, people got somewhere to stay. The workhouse provided poor-quality food such as gruel, a kind of watery porridge, along with old clothes and medical care. All kinds of people went to the workhouse, including orphans, children abandoned by their parents, the mentally ill, the disabled, elderly people, and unmarried women. Life was not easy in the workhouse, but it was better than living on the streets.

Workhouses were often crowded and uncomfortable, like prisons.

As Britain became more industrialized and richer, the question about the best way to deal with the growing numbers of the poor became more urgent. The government passed different laws to try to solve the issue, but not all of them helped the poor. In 1834, the Poor Law was amended to say that parishes no longer had to help anyone who refused to move into the workhouse. That left thousands of people desperately poor.

This photograph shows workhouse children in northern England in the late 1800s.

# VICTORIAN CHILDREN

The new factories built in the mid-1800s required so many workers that even children went to work. Some were only four years old. Children could do jobs that adults were too big for, such as crawling into small gaps in coal mines. There were no laws limiting the number of hours anyone could work. Some children worked 16 hours a day, often in dangerous conditions. Inside factories, they did jobs from making matches and nails to crawling under machines to collect waste material. Outside factories, children worked as chimney sweeps, servants, coal miners, or delivery boys and girls.

*... even children went to work.*

As public outrage about child labor grew, Parliament passed two bills to control it. In 1833, the Factory Act limited the age a child could work to 9 years and older and limited the number of hours a child under 13 could work. The Mines Act of 1842 banned children from working in coal mines until they were 10 years old. Both of these laws helped children but did not stop child labor.

For Charles Dickens, the difficulties faced by young people were a major concern. In many of his novels, including *Oliver Twist*, *Dombey and Son*, and *Bleak House*, he writes about the harsh lives of young orphans and child workers.

## Words that changed the world

In Bleak House, *Jo is described with these words, "He is not softened by distance and unfamiliarity; he is not a genuine foreign-grown savage; he is the ordinary homemade article. Dirty, ugly, disagreeable to all the senses, in body a common creature of the common streets, only in soul a heathen. Homely filth begrimes him, homely parasites devour him, homely sores are in him, homely rags are on him; native ignorance, the growth of English soil and climate, sinks his immortal nature lower than the beasts that perish. Stand forth, Jo, in uncompromising colours! From the sole of thy foot to the crown of thy head, there is nothing interesting about thee."*

## Exploring the text

In this text, Dickens describes Jo, a crossing sweeper. Homeless and with no family, Jo earns a small amount of money sweeping a path across streets so that people can walk without getting their shoes dirty. Eventually, he dies of pneumonia—and no one notices.

Young boys worked in coal mines moving heavy loads.

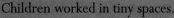

Children worked in tiny spaces.

# HISTORY'S STORY

Dickens spent many hours wandering around London. He walked miles through the streets, noticing things that most people did not. Although Jo is a minor character in *Bleak House*, Dickens wants his reader to feel pity for him and his tough life. For Dickens, Jo stands for all the poor children whom nobody notices.

# TIMELINE OF THE INDUSTRIAL REVOLUTION

**1764** James Hargreaves develops the Spinning Jenny. This machine speeds up cotton spinning.

**1769** Richard Arkwright invents the water frame. This allows cotten spinning to be done by machines.

**1769** James Watt refines a steam engine. The engine is the main source of power that drives new machines.

**1785** The power loom is invented. Used with the steam engine's power, it transforms the cotton industry.

**1801** A steam-powered locomotive is invented for use on the highway.

Power looms for weaving cotton were gathered together in large factories called mills.

The Great Exhibition was held in 1851 to show the world the power of Britain's economy and industry.

**1812** The British parliament passes a law making it punishable by death to destroy industrial machines.

**1814** George Stephenson invents a steam-engine locomotive to run on rails.

**1826** George Stephenson wins the commission to build 30 miles (48 km) of railroad tracks between Liverpool and Manchester.

**1829** George Stephenson's locomotive *Rocket* wins a speed competition. The Liverpool–Manchester railroad is completed.

**1835** There are 106,000 power looms operating in Britain's cotton mills.

**1851** The Great Exhibition in the Crystal Palace in London shows off manufactured goods from throughout Britain's worldwide empire.

# CHAPTER 3

A young actor plays Oliver

## OLIVER TWIST
### Masterwork

**Key facts about *Oliver Twist*:**

**Full title:** *Oliver Twist or The Parish Boy's Progress*

**First appeared:** *Bentley's Miscellany*, 1837–1839

**Published under the name of:** Boz

**Published as a novel:** 1839

**Hero:** Oliver Twist

**What's the story?:** The novel tells the story of the orphan Oliver Twist's journey from the workhouse to London, and how he falls in with a criminal group, led by the criminal Fagin, but eventually achieves a happy life.

*Oliver Twist*
is a POWERFUL tale
of GRIEF, TRIAL, and
SORROW in nineteenth-
century Britain. In Dickens's
words, "… if it were one
of unmixed JOY and
HAPPINESS, it would
be very BRIEF."

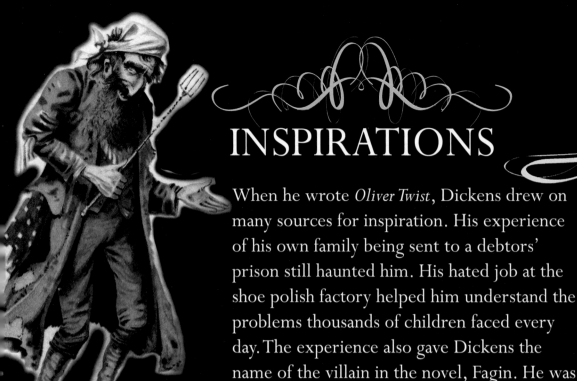

# INSPIRATIONS

When he wrote *Oliver Twist*, Dickens drew on many sources for inspiration. His experience of his own family being sent to a debtors' prison still haunted him. His hated job at the shoe polish factory helped him understand the problems thousands of children faced every day. The experience also gave Dickens the name of the villain in the novel, Fagin. He was named for his friend at the factory, Bob Fagin.

Fagin is one of the only truly evil characters Dickens describes in the novel.

During the 1830s, a book named *A Memoir of Robert Blincoe* became very popular. The book was an account of Blincoe's real life as an orphan in a workhouse. At six years old, he was put to work as a chimney sweep, and at seven, he went to work in a mill. Years of working in the mill left him stunted and with crooked legs. The book described the horrible working conditions in the cotton mills. Shortly after it was published, the government launched a study into conditions there.

*The book described the horrible working conditions in the cotton mills.*

Another inspiration was the children Dickens saw around him every day on the streets of London. There were children everywhere, many of whom were homeless or living in workhouses. To make a living, many of them became pickpockets. They stole anything they could. Silk handkerchiefs were very popular, because they were easy to sell.

## Words that changed the world

*In Oliver Twist, Dickens described the terror Oliver experiences on the streets of London: "'Stop thief! Stop thief!' There is a passion for hunting something deeply implanted in the human breast. One wretched, breathless child, panting with exhaustion, terror in his looks, agony in his eye, large drops of perspiration streaming down his face, strains every nerve to make head upon his pursuers; and as they follow on his track, and gain upon him every instant, they hail his decreasing strength with still louder shouts, and whoop and scream with joy. 'Stop thief!'"*

## Exploring the text

In this text, Oliver is on his first outing as part of Fagin's gang of pickpockets. He is being chased by a large crowd who believe he has stolen a gentleman's handkerchief. The experience is so terrifying that Dickens says it would be a relief, or mercy, if someone stopped him. In fact, two other boys from Fagin's gang have carried out the crime. Unable to run as fast as the adults, Oliver is soon captured.

Oliver runs through the street as he tries to escape from an angry mob who believe he is a thief.

## HISTORY'S STORY

Dickens describes Oliver's terror as he tries to escape. Throughout the book, he shows sympathy for the young pickpockets, such as the Artful Dodger. He wants his reader to understand how poverty impacted children with no parents to look after them. Crime was often the only way children could care for themselves.

# WRITING
## *OLIVER TWIST*

Charles Dickens published *Oliver Twist* in monthly installments in the magazine *Bentley's Miscellany*. He was also the magazine's editor, which meant he was responsible for finding other stories to fill its pages.

Unlike with his first novel, *The Pickwick Papers*, Dickens already knew how *Oliver Twist* would end before he started writing it. He had the idea for the story as early as December 1833, but the first installment did not appear for over three years. Before the novel finished its magazine run, it was published as a single book. The front cover gave the author's name as "Boz," the name Dickens had first used for his short stories.

### Providing the illustrations

To accompany Dickens's text, each installment also had a drawing by the illustrator George Cruikshank. Cruikshank was a friend of Dickens who had illustrated Dickens's earliest work, *Sketches by Boz* (1836). The book was full of descriptions of scenes in London. Cruikshank drew engravings. He worked by scratching a drawing on a plate of copper, which was then covered in ink and printed. Cruikshank had to create the drawing in reverse so that when it printed it was the right way around. Cruikshank was already famous for his cartoons, which made fun of the upper levels of British society. King George IV was said to have paid Cruikshank to get him to stop drawing cartoons mocking the king.

George Cruikshank made his name with cartoons like this one poking fun at contemporary fashions.

## A falling-out

Dickens and Cruikshank eventually fell out. Cruikshank claimed that he had come up with much of the plot for *Oliver Twist*. He said Dickens had used his ideas. Dickens rejected the claim.

When Dickens started writing *Oliver Twist*, he was still finishing *The Pickwick Papers*. The two books were very different, but Dickens was able to switch between the two easily. He went from writing funny episodes to heartbreaking accounts of poverty, sometimes in the same day.

## HISTORY'S STORY

George Cruikshank belonged to a long line of illustrators who used their drawings to make satirical comments about life. In the 1700s, William Hogarth had poked fun at all aspects of daily life. Cruikshank's own father, Isaac, had also been a famous cartoonist. Cartoons were particularly popular with the many people who could not read.

# PLOT BREAKDOWN

*Oliver Twist* tells the story of the orphaned Oliver and how he goes from the workhouse to a life of crime until he is finally rescued and leaves London for a happy life. Along the way, he encounters a wide range of characters and adventures.

Oliver's mother dies giving birth to him. The boy never finds out who his father is. For the first nine years of his life, he lives in a home for orphans before being sent to a workhouse. Hungry, one day he asks for more food. As a punishment, he is sent from the workhouse to work for an undertaker, Mr. Sowerberry. After his dead mother is insulted, Oliver runs away to London.

## Joining the gang

In London, the child is taken in by a criminal gang of young pickpockets led by Fagin. The gang teaches Oliver how to pick the pockets of gentlemen for silk handkerchiefs. On his first pickpocketing mission, Oliver is caught and narrowly avoids being sent to jail. Mr. Brownlow, the gentleman whose handkerchief is stolen, takes him in.

Oliver asks for more food from the master in a famous scene near the beginning of the novel.

Mr. Brownlow thinks Oliver looks just like the portrait of a lady that he has in his home. Oliver's happy stay in Mr. Brownlow's house ends when he is kidnapped by two members of Fagin's gang and taken back to Fagin.

## A kidnap plot

Forced to rob a house, Oliver is shot and wounded. This time he is taken in by Mrs. Maylie and her adopted niece, Rose, the people he attempted to rob. He spends the summer with them, but Fagin is determined to get him back.

Oliver is kidnapped by the mysterious Monks.

By now, Fagin is being helped by a mysterious man named Monks, who seems to be related to Oliver. Monks obtains a locket that contains a portrait of Oliver's parents, but he destroys it. Meanwhile, the plot to kidnap Oliver is discovered by Nancy, a member of Fagin's gang. Nancy warns the Maylies that Oliver is in danger. For betraying the plot, she is brutally murdered by her partner, Bill Sikes.

The Maylies reunite Oliver with Mr. Brownlow, who confronts Monks. He finds out that Monks is Oliver's half brother. Monks has been chasing Oliver to make sure that he does not inherit his share of their father's fortune. Brownlow forces Monks to sign over Oliver's share so that the boy will have money in the future. Rose turns out to be the younger sister of Oliver's mother, making her Oliver's aunt. Fagin is hanged for his crimes. Mr. Brownlow adopts Oliver and they move to the countryside near the Maylies, far away from the crime of London.

# KEY CHARACTERS IN *OLIVER TWIST*

Oliver Twist

**Oliver Twist**    The story's hero is an orphan who survives the workhouse and working for Fagin's criminal gang before his true identity is finally revealed and he gets the happy life he deserves.

**Fagin**    A career criminal who recruits Oliver to his criminal gang of child thieves. Fagin is hanged for his crimes.

**Nancy**    A woman who works for Fagin. She is a kind person who is murdered by her boyfriend, Bill Sikes, for trying to help Oliver.

**Rose Maylie**    Raised by Mrs. Maylie, she turns out to be Oliver's aunt, as she is the sister of his dead mother, Agnes Fleming.

**Mr. Brownlow**

A gentleman who takes Oliver under his wing. He has a portrait of Oliver's mother in his home.

**Monks**

A nasty man who works with Fagin. He turns out to be the half brother of Oliver, whom he wants to disinherit.

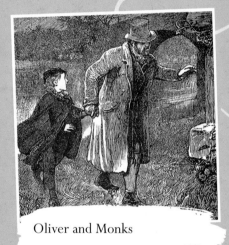

Oliver and Monks

**Bill Sikes**

One of Fagin's gang, he is a burglar known for his cruelty. He is Nancy's boyfriend. After he murders her, he dies trying to escape a mob.

**The Artful Dodger**

His real name is Jack Dawkins. He is the smartest of Fagin's pickpockets. He introduces Oliver to Fagin.

**Mr. Sowerberry**

The undertaker Oliver works for after he leaves the workhouse. Sowerberry is kind to Oliver, but Sowerberry's wife and apprentice are mean to him.

# CHAPTER 4

This image shows a slum in London.

## OLIVER TWIST
### Key Themes

**Major themes of *Oliver Twist*:**

Good versus evil

Justice versus injustice

Law versus crime

Country versus town

Cruelty versus kindness

Poor versus rich

Family versus orphans

**Overview:** *Oliver Twist* is a type of story called a morality tale. It shows that acting in a moral way is rewarded, while those who act badly suffer for their actions. By staying true to goodness, Oliver eventually gets the life he wants and a happy ending despite the terrible things that happen to him along the way.

*Morals* were very IMPORTANT in Victorian SOCIETY. Dickens shows this CLEARLY in *Oliver Twist*, in which we SEE that if a PERSON has a GOOD HEART and STRIVES to do GOOD, his actions will LEAD to a BETTER LIFE.

# THE POOR LAW

The first part of *Oliver Twist* takes place in the workhouse where Oliver is sent at the age of nine. This gave Dickens the opportunity to criticize a law that had been introduced in 1834, two years before he began writing the novel.

This cartoon shows an angel crying as a woman is taken away to the workhouse.

The Poor Law Amendment Act was introduced to change the Poor Law of 1815. The original law had made each parish responsible for helping the poor by giving them money, food, or accommodation if they could not work. Parishes complained that this was very expensive. The aim of the new act was to reduce the amount of money spent on the poor. The new act said that the poor must work in workhouses in exchange for food and a place to stay. Each parish had a board of guardians to decide who deserved to be helped. These guardians were usually local landowners.

*... the poor must work in workhouses in exchange for food ...*

Dickens was among many people who thought the new act treated the poor badly. He did not like the fact that a group of wealthy people got to decide who was helped and who was not. He also thought that the conditions in workhouses were too harsh. Food was terrible and children, in particular, were treated cruelly. Workhouse children were commonly thin and starving.

## Words that changed the world

*In* Oliver Twist, *Dickens shows the cruelty experienced by the poor when Oliver asks for more food:* "'Please, sir, I want some more.' The master was a fat, healthy man; but he turned very pale. He gazed in stupefied astonishment on the small rebel for some seconds, and then clung for support to the copper. The assistants were paralyzed with wonder; the boys with fear. 'What!' said the master at length, in a faint voice. 'Please, sir,' replied Oliver, 'I want some more.' The master aimed a blow at Oliver's head with the ladle; pinioned him in his arm; and shrieked aloud for the beadle."

The other boys look on as Oliver asks the master for more gruel.

## Exploring the text

When Oliver asks for more gruel, the master is angry. Dickens emphasizes the master's fat body as a way of contrasting it with the hunger of the boys. Dickens wants his reader to understand the unfairness of the workhouse system. The workhouse food is not nutritious and the boys are hungry. The horrified reaction of the master, and later of the board of guardians, suggests that they do not think of the poor as other human beings but as grasping, greedy individuals.

## HISTORY'S STORY

Later in his career, Dickens set up an alternative to a workhouse. He worked with an heiress named Angela Burdett-Coutts to help homeless women. They founded a home called Urania Cottage. Women lived there while they were trained and educated so they could have a future.

# THE WORKING CLASS

Much of the action of *Oliver Twist* takes place in overcrowded slums in London's East End. The houses are dirty and flea-ridden, with many families living in one shabby room. The people cannot read or write, and most of them do not have any training or skills. A lack of money means they cannot eat healthy food. This means that many of them get sick. Many working-class families have a lot of children, so they can be sent out to earn money as soon as they are old enough.

Many children in *Oliver Twist* are orphans. Without any family to look after them, they often end up in the workhouse. Oliver meets many other boys at the workhouse who are in the same position as him. The workhouse offers them no future. For Oliver, Fagin and Fagin's gang seem to be his only chance of becoming part of a kind of family. However, this comes at the price of becoming a criminal. As Dickens shows, some young people saw this as their only opportunity to make any money and improve their lives.

This painting contrasts the lives of a poor couple (left) with that of a wealthy man.

## Social contrast

In contrast, Dickens paints a picture of the wealthy as being comfortable. They have plenty of food, and clean places to live. The board of guardians and the master of the workhouse are well fed. Mr. Brownlow and the Maylies are well dressed and enjoy the finer things in life. They live outside London, because Dickens suggests that the countryside is a healthier environment than the city. The air is clean and wholesome in contrast to the dirt of the city.

Poor Londoners stand in line to get drinking water from a pump in the street.

Dickens also suggests that moving between social classes in nineteenth-century Britain is almost impossible. Throughout the story, people remark that Oliver has some quality that suggests he was born into a better social class. However, the fact that his mother was not married to his father means that he is socially unacceptable. It is only when Mr. Brownlow adopts him that Oliver is accepted into the middle class.

## HISTORY'S STORY

Discussions about the poor in the 1800s became known as the "Condition of England" debate. The writer Thomas Carlyle came up with the phrase in 1839. It described different ideas about an industrial, urban society. Dickens, like Carlyle, thought rapid industrialization had made the lives of the poor almost unimaginably hard. Dickens used his novels to highlight their plight.

# LAW AND ORDER

One of the major themes of *Oliver Twist* is the lack of law and order in London. This is most clearly expressed in the central role of Fagin's gang. The gang steals from people in the streets and robs houses while the occupants sleep. The fear of crime was high, and particularly of the theft of property.

Dickens was not alone in being concerned about the problem. In 1829, the home secretary, Sir Robert Peel, created the Metropolitan Police. It was London's first full-time professional, centrally organized police force. It was part of a campaign to improve public order on London's streets.

*Oliver Twist* clearly showed that the new police force was necessary. Dickens introduces all kinds of criminals, including pickpockets, murderers, and burglars. They congregate in crime-ridden slums known as "rookeries." Dickens shows how poverty and a lack of education have led many of his characters into a life of crime.

Two policemen arrest a suspect at night in a men's hostel in London.

## Crime and punishment

Newspapers reported crimes every day, often carried out by children as young as seven. As *Oliver Twist* reveals, one of the most popular things to steal was the silk handkerchiefs gentlemen carried in their pockets. In that way, handkerchiefs were similar to the cell phones of today. They were easy to resell and were worth a relatively high price. Up to 5,000 handkerchiefs a week were handled in Field Lane, the real street in which Dickens located Fagin's criminal den.

For people caught stealing, the punishment could be harsh. Theft could be punished by death. Even children were sentenced to death by the British courts for stealing, although these sentences were not carried out. Adults were not so lucky. They were often hanged in public executions that attracted many spectators. Two-thirds of the 671 hangings carried out in Great Britain in the 1820s were for theft. Only one-fifth were for murder.

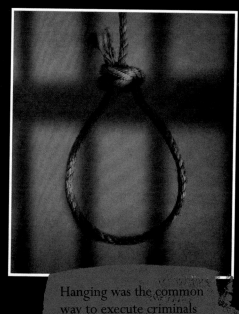

Hanging is mentioned often in *Oliver Twist*. The threat of being hanged is used to scare Oliver. Even his name, "Twist," is a slang word for being hanged. The only two purely evil criminals Dickens describes in the book are Fagin and Bill Sikes. Both die by hanging. Fagin is executed in a public hanging while Sikes accidentally falls and hangs himself while trying to escape from an angry mob.

Hanging was the common way to execute criminals in Victorian Britain.

# DICKENS'S MAJOR WORKS AND THEIR THEMES

### Nicholas Nickleby (1838)

This novel looks at the terrible conditions of boys' boarding schools in northern England.

### A Christmas Carol (1843)

This is an exploration of poverty versus wealth and meanness versus generosity.

### David Copperfield (1849)

This looks at attachment versus loss, good versus evil, and the damaging effects of wealth and class.

### Bleak House (1852)

This novel explores the search for love and the importance of passion and its dangers, as well as the urgent need for reform of the outdated British legal system.

### Hard Times (1854)

This explores harmful effects of the Industrial Revolution.

An illustration from
*David Copperfield*

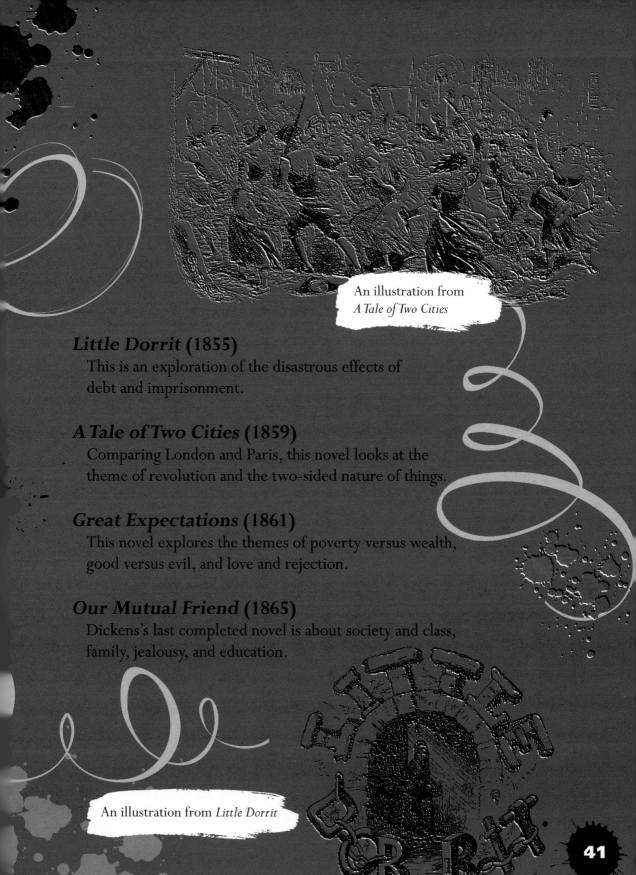

An illustration from
*A Tale of Two Cities*

## Little Dorrit (1855)

This is an exploration of the disastrous effects of debt and imprisonment.

## A Tale of Two Cities (1859)

Comparing London and Paris, this novel looks at the theme of revolution and the two-sided nature of things.

## Great Expectations (1861)

This novel explores the themes of poverty versus wealth, good versus evil, and love and rejection.

## Our Mutual Friend (1865)

Dickens's last completed novel is about society and class, family, jealousy, and education.

An illustration from *Little Dorrit*

# CHAPTER 5

A soup kitchen for poor children

## STIRRING REFORM
### Effecting Change

### Key reformations in Britain:

In a period of rapid change as Britain industrialized, its lawmakers in Parliament passed many different acts to address the difficulties and problems within society created by the new industries.

### Reforms included:

Factory Acts, 1833, 1844, 1847

Mines and Collieries Act, 1842

Education Act, 1880

Public Health Act, 1848

Sanitation Act, 1866

*Dickens* was a HUGELY important FIGURE of his TIME. His NOVELS and CAMPAIGNING for SOCIAL JUSTICE helped pave the way for many acts of SOCIAL REFORMATION. By SHINING a LIGHT on the PLIGHT of the POOR, Dickens helped FORCE change for the BETTER in Victorian SOCIETY.

# A CONTINUING CAMPAIGN

After *Oliver Twist*, Dickens used many of his later novels to address different social issues that concerned him and other social reformers. He was particularly interested in what he saw as the negative impact of the rapid growth of cities and factories on ordinary people. The squalor and poverty of the working class and the seeming lack of understanding of the rich underlies much of Dickens's writing.

In *Bleak House* (1852), Dickens describes a foggy London in which everything is hidden and clouded. He uses the fog as a symbol to suggest that the city is being choked to death. The complex legal system and greedy businesses are sucking out its life. The novel concentrates on the growing inequality of life. It contrasts the poor housing, disease-ridden slums, and the lack of opportunity for the poor with the lazy and rich lawyers, preachers, and businesspeople who share the same city.

*… the city is slowly being choked to death.*

In *Hard Times* (1854), Dickens shows what happens to workers in his fictional town of Coketown as a result of industrialization and urbanization. At the same time, he examines how divided the social classes are becoming. He depicts the terrible conditions for laborers, their lack of education in anything other than basic facts, and the lack of any pleasure or kindness in their lives. Dickens makes it clear that he believes that unrestrained capitalism has destroyed much that is good in human society.

## Words that changed the world

*In* The Life and Adventures of Nicholas Nickleby, *Dickens wrote,"There were little faces which should have been handsome, darkened with the scowl of sullen, dogged suffering; there was childhood with the light of its eye quenched, its beauty gone, and its helplessness alone remaining; there were vicious-faced boys, brooding, with leaden eyes, like malefactors in a jail ...With every kindly sympathy and affection blasted in its birth, with every young and healthy feeling flogged and starved down, with every revengeful passion that can fester in swollen hearts, eating its evil way to their core in silence, what an incipient Hell was breeding here!"*

*Bleak House* uses the symbol of London's thick fog to show how the city is choked by the legal system.

## Exploring the text

In *The Life and Adventures of Nicholas Nickleby* (1838), Dickens continues his work to raise awareness of widespread child suffering in Victorian England. This time, his concern was to expose the boarding schools to which many unwanted children were sent, particularly in the north of England. These schools were little better than the workhouses. This excerpt describes the unlucky boys who are students at Dotheboys Hall. Like other schools, it was run for profit with no regard for the benefit of students. Dickens says that the school has changed the boys for the worse, so they end up looking like prisoners. He points out that the schooling is storing up problems for the future by creating vicious, revengeful adults.

# CAUSING OUTRAGE

The Condition of England was the name given by the Scottish writer Thomas Carlyle to the debate about the social changes taking place in the Industrial Revolution. While a large part of the population was growing rich and living more comfortably, their comfort was based on the suffering of the poorest members of society. Dickens was a great admirer of Carlyle. He based *A Tale of Two Cities* on Carlyle's writings about the French Revolution.

Dickens, Carlyle, and other social reformers believed that the Industrial Revolution had created an England of two nations. Carlyle wrote a number of books to raise awareness about the gap between rich and poor and to suggest how it might be bridged. Dickens took Carlyle's ideas and turned them into fiction.

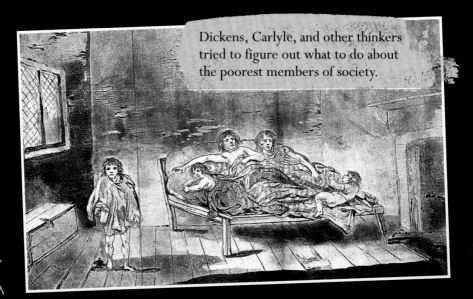

Dickens, Carlyle, and other thinkers tried to figure out what to do about the poorest members of society.

In *Oliver Twist* and later novels, Dickens showed readers what happens to the majority of the population when a relatively few people control most of the wealth through their factories, mills, and mines. Carlyle and Dickens did not think that poverty was inevitable. They believed that reform was possible if business leaders changed how they acted. Dickens believed the government had to take the lead and pass laws to help the poor. In the same way, he believed the rich and fortunate had a responsibility to help those who were less fortunate.

Carlyle argued that the Industrial Revolution was turning people into machines. Industrial work stripped them of their individuality and personality. Dickens agreed. In *Hard Times*, he even describes the factory workers as "the Hands"—because that is the only part of them needed to do factory work.

Dickens also satirizes some of the preachers and moral do-gooders who claim to help the poor. Such people lecture the poor about how to achieve spiritual salvation, despite their material poverty. In *Bleak House*, a preacher visits a poor brickmaker and lectures him about accepting his lot in life. The brickmaker asks what the point is of any moral cleanliness in the face of a filthy cottage.

## HISTORY'S STORY

Not everyone shared Dickens's belief that the government should improve the lives of the poor. Some people argued that individuals were responsible for themselves and had to make their own way in the world. They suggested that the poor brought poverty on themselves by being lazy or having poor morals.

# SOCIAL REFORM

Dickens's popularity allowed him to draw attention to social issues in Great Britain and the United States. In 1853, he published *A Christmas Carol*. This famous novella, or short novel, told the story of Scrooge, a miserly old man who refused to celebrate Christmas. The book helped change the way people behaved by pointing out how people had lost their sense of charity. After the book's publication, charities in Britain noticed

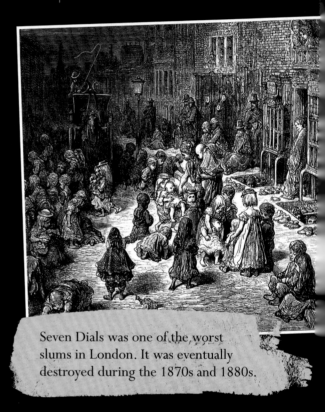

Seven Dials was one of the worst slums in London. It was eventually destroyed during the 1870s and 1880s.

a rise in the donations they received. One factory owner in the United States gave all his workers a turkey for Christmas.

Meanwhile, pressure from Dickens and other social reformers was beginning to get the government to try to solve some of the worst problems of the time. The British parliament passed a series of laws to try to improve the working conditions of factory and mine workers.

New laws limited the hours women and children could work. Sometimes reforms had a negative effect, however. In 1842, the Mines and Collieries Act banned women and children from working in mines. The act led to higher levels of unemployment and greater hardship among some families.

While Dickens's novels gave his readers a human view of society's problems, other reformers took a more scientific approach. In 1842, Edwin Chadwick wrote *Report on Sanitary Conditions of the Labouring Population of Great Britain*. Chadwick methodically recorded the conditions he found in different parts of the country. He argued that disease was caused by poverty and that only by making the homes of the poor cleaner and by cleaning up the cities would society get rid of deadly diseases, such as cholera. His work and the work of others eventually led to the 1866 Sanitation Act, which ordered the destruction and replacement of slum dwellings.

For his part, Dickens wanted to contribute to social reform beyond his writings. He opened Urania Cottage in London in May 1846. Dickens and his partner in the venture, Angela Burdett-Coutts, believed strongly that homeless women should be given a second chance. By providing accommodation and training, he hoped that women would have a better future. More than 100 women were helped at Urania Cottage between 1847 and 1859.

## HISTORY'S STORY

One reason social reform was slow was that most people could not vote. The Reform Act of 1832 expanded the right to vote, but only one man in seven could vote, and no women. Elections were dominated by wealthy voters. The poorest had no say. Even by the end of the 1800s, about 40 percent of men were still unable to take part in elections. British women did not get the vote until 1918.

# TIMELINE OF SOCIAL CHANGE IN GREAT BRITAIN

**1833** Factory Act—improves conditions for children working in factories.

**1833** Slavery Abolition Act—bans slavery throughout the British Empire.

**1834** Poor Law Amendment Act—requires poor people to go to workhouses to get help.

**1839** Child Custody Act—gives mothers custody of children in the case of divorce or death.

**1842** Mines & Collieries Act— keeps women and children from working in coal mines.

This image shows protestors calling for social change in London in 1848.

After 1842, children under 10 years old were forbidden to work in coal mines.

**1844** Ragged Schools Union—Dickens supports this organization that provides education for poor children.

**1844** Factory Act—forces machinery to be fenced off and forbids children to clean it while it is still working.

**1847** Factory Act, or the Ten Hours Act—limits the working hours of women and young adults aged 13 to 18.

**1848** Public Health Act—improves sanitation in order to reduce the spread of deadly diseases.

**1857** Marriage Act—gives women more rights within marriage.

**1866** Sanitation Act—begins the process of the removal and improvement of slum dwellings.

**1878** Factory and Workshops Act—limits women to working 60 hours a week and forbids children under 10 from working altogether.

**1880** Education Act—makes going to school mandatory for children between ages 5 and 10.

# CHAPTER 6

Dickens in his study

# DICKENS'S LEGACY
## Aftermath

**Novels published:**

1837 *The Pickwick Papers*

1839 *Oliver Twist*

1838 *Nicholas Nickleby*

1841 *The Old Curiosity Shop*

1841 *Barnaby Rudge*

1844 *Martin Chuzzlewit*

1848 *Dombey and Son*

1849 *David Copperfield*

1852 *Bleak House*

1854 *Hard Times*

1855 *Little Dorrit*

1859 *A Tale of Two Cities*

1861 *Great Expectations*

1865 *Our Mutual Friend*

1870 *The Mystery of Edwin Drood*

**Best-selling novels in Dickens's lifetime**

1. *Bleak House*

2. *Dombey and Son*

3. *Little Dorrit*

*A Tale of Two Cities* has sold more than 200 million copies.

*The* NOVELS of Charles Dickens have stood the TEST of TIME and are as popular TODAY as they were at the time they were PUBLISHED. For modern readers, the works open a WINDOW into the INDUSTRIAL AGE, and in the writer's WORDS reveal that it was "the spring of HOPE, it was the winter of DESPAIR."

# END OF A LONG CAREER

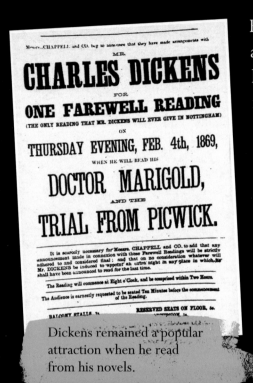

Messrs. CHAPPELL and CO. beg to announce that they have made arrangements with

MR.
## CHARLES DICKENS

FOR

## ONE FAREWELL READING

(THE ONLY READING THAT MR. DICKENS WILL EVER GIVE IN NOTTINGHAM)

ON

### THURSDAY EVENING, FEB. 4th, 1869,

WHEN HE WILL READ HIS

## DOCTOR MARIGOLD,

AND THE

## TRIAL FROM PICWICK.

It is scarcely necessary for Messrs. CHAPPELL and CO. to add that any announcement made in connexion with these Farewell Readings will be strictly adhered to and considered final; and that on no consideration whatever will Mr. DICKENS be induced to "appoint" an extra night in any place in which he shall have been announced to read for the last time.

The Reading will commence at Eight o'Clock, and be comprised within Two Hours.

The Audience is earnestly requested to be seated Ten Minutes before the commencement of the Reading.

BALCONY STALLS. 7s.                    RESERVED SEATS ON FLOOR, 5s.

Dickens remained a popular attraction when he read from his novels.

By the 1840s, Charles Dickens was rich and successful. He was the greatest living author, and had become highly influential. Dickens continued to work on his novels throughout the 1840s and 1850s. Even when his father died in 1851 and his own ninth child suddenly died, he kept on working. By 1855, he was rich enough to buy a house he had seen as a child, on Gad's Hill in Chatham. He would live there until his death in 1870.

*He was the greatest living author.*

As well as writing his novels, Dickens found time to start his own monthly magazines. First, he started *Household Words*, which published stories by his friends, the writers William Thackeray and Wilkie Collins. He and Collins wrote a play called *The Frozen Deep* about the last days of English explorers who got lost in the Arctic in 1845. Dickens also directed the play. After he shut down *Household Words*, he started another magazine, *All the Year Round*, in which he serialized his novel about the French Revolution, *A Tale of Two Cities*.

In addition, Dickens continued to tour around Great Britain giving readings from his novels. In 1867, he sailed to the United States for a second tour. This time the tour was a triumph. Dickens met many fans, including President Andrew Johnson, who invited Dickens to the White House.

Dickens died peacefully at home at Gad's Hill after he suffered a stroke. He was 58 years old.

Constant work took its toll on Dickens's health, which had never been great. He pushed himself until his death on June 9, 1870. His last novel, *The Mystery of Edwin Drood*, was left unfinished. Dickens was buried in Poet's Corner in Westminster Abbey, London, in recognition of his place as one of the greatest writers England has ever produced.

## Words that changed the world

*In* David Copperfield, *Mr. Micawber discusses money with the following words :"Annual income twenty pounds, annual expenditure nineteen [pounds] nineteen [shillings] and six [pence], result happiness. Annual income twenty pounds, annual expenditure twenty pounds ought and six, result misery."*

## Exploring the text

Mr. Micawber is a clerk in *David Copperfield*. He is an eternal optimist. He spends more than he earns because he constantly expects his luck to turn and money to turn up. Dickens based the character of Mr. Micawber on his own father, John. Mr. Micawber understands how to make his life less stressful, but he does not follow his own advice and is therefore constantly in debt. *David Copperfield* was so popular that "Micawber" became a popular term for someone who always owed money but did not worry because they thought that something would turn up.

# MAKING A
# DIFFERENCE

Dickens lived during a period known as the Great Reform. It took its name from the improvements the British government made to try to protect people from the worst effects of industrialization. Dickens used his novels to highlight social issues he felt needed to be addressed. The government responded to some of the issues—but not all of them.

Dickens's chief concern was the plight of children and the problems families faced when they lacked money. The memory of his family's stay in the debtors' prison never left Dickens. Both *Little Dorrit* and *David Copperfield* describe families in debt. He also devoted himself to helping women. *Dombey and Son* illustrates the short-sightedness of men who do not consider women their equals. During the 1800s, many people began to argue that women should be treated more equally by the law. In 1857, the Marriage Act was passed to give women more equality with their husbands within their marriage.

Dickens revealed how difficult life was for most people in Britain's cities. Unable to escape their plight because of poverty and a lack of education, millions lived in squalor that Dickens revealed for the first time.

In the late 1800s, local councils began to build better homes for the poor.

An association was set up to improve health in towns throughout Great Britain.

Many of Dickens's readers were shocked to learn that Jacob's Island, where Bill Sikes lives in *Oliver Twist*, was a real place. It was a slum on the south bank of the River Thames in London. In response to reports linking disease with dirty living conditions, the government passed laws to improve sanitation in the cities. It also began knocking down some of the worst slums.

Industry spread rapidly, especially in the north of England. Thousands of factories and mills were built, and small towns grew into large cities. Men, women, and children did hard, mindless jobs in factories where they rarely saw daylight. Dickens captured the horror of this new world in *Hard Times*. The government recognized the terrible working conditions and passed laws to limit the working day and who could work in the mines and factories.

## HISTORY'S STORY

Dickens was very popular in the United States, where he made two long visits in 1842 and 1867. Opposed to the rigid British class system, he was eager to see if American democracy offered a fairer way to live. For their part, the Americans loved Dickens's novels. On his second trip, he was welcomed as a superstar.

# AN ENDURING
# POPULARITY

Dickens is still read today around the world. His books have never gone out of print. Since his novels were first published, his stories have gripped the imagination of millions of readers. Dickens often read from his works and turned his readings into theatrical events. On his farewell reading tours in 1868 and 1869, he read from *A Christmas Carol* and *The Pickwick Papers*.

Dickens did not just read his work out loud on stage, he also acted out some of his most famous characters. In 1868, he surprised his friends with his performance as Bill Sikes, the murderer from *Oliver Twist*. His acting was so terrifying that some members of the audience fainted. *The Frozen Deep*, the play he wrote with Wilkie Collins, was such a hit that Dickens performed it in front of Queen Victoria.

Dickens loved acting and appeared on the stage in plays and reading his own work.

## Plays and movies

Some of Dickens's novels were turned into plays during his lifetime. Since his death in 1870, many more have been staged as plays. Some, such as *Nicholas Nickleby* and *Oliver Twist*, have been turned into long-running musicals. *Oliver!*, the musical based on *Oliver Twist*, was first staged in 1960 and is still performed across the globe. Almost all of Dickens's novels have been turned into movies, most more than once. There is a version of most of his novels for every generation. *A Christmas Carol* has been made into a movie many times, into a cartoon, and has even been turned into a Muppet movie.

An actor appears on stage dressed as Fagin during a performance of the musical *Oliver!*

Dickens has remained popular and topical because many of the issues he dealt with in the 1800s still exist today. Many children across the world still live in poverty and are forced to work instead of playing or going to school. Many workers still face unsafe conditions. There is still great inequality in the world and poverty destroys the lives of millions of people. Dickens's themes and characters are still relevant today. In many ways, he was the first writer of the modern age.

## HISTORY'S STORY

Since Dickens wrote *Oliver Twist*, some things have changed. In the first editions of the novel, Dickens often called Fagin simply "the Jew." Dickens denied that this was anti-Semitic. In a later edition, however, he took out a lot of the references. Today, it is unacceptable to refer to a person's religion as a means of criticizing them.

# OTHER NOVELISTS WHO BROUGHT REFORM

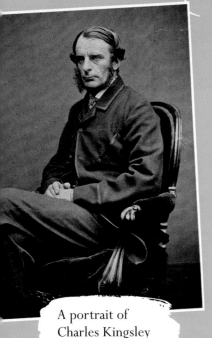

A portrait of
Charles Kingsley

### Charles Kingsley (1819–1875)

*Alton Locke* (1850) is a novel about social injustice.
*The Water Babies: A Fairy Tale for a Land Baby* (1863)
attacks child labor, particularly child chimney sweeps.

### Elizabeth Gaskell (1810–1865)

*Mary Barton* (1848) is about relations between
workers and employers.
*North and South* (1854) describes the lives of workers
and their relationships with their employers.

### Charlotte Brontë (1816-1855)

*Shirley* (1849) describes the Luddite uprisings, in
which textile workers smashed the machines they
feared would put them out of work.

A scene from *Mary Barton*

SYBIL;

OR,

THE TWO NATIONS.

BY

B. DISRAELI, M.P.

AUTHOR OF "CONINGSBY."

"The Commonalty murmured, and said, 'There never were so many Gentlemen, and so little Gentleness.'"—BISHOP LATIMER.

IN THREE VOLS.

VOL. I.

The title-page of *Sybil*

## Benjamin Disraeli (1804–1881) British prime minister

*Sybil, or The Two Nations* (1845) looks at the terrible conditions of the working classes.

## Caroline Norton (1808-1877)

*Stuart of Dunleath* (1851) highlights the difficulties of a woman who is controlled by her mean husband.

A portrait of Caroline Norton

# GLOSSARY

**amended** changed

**apprentice** a person who is learning how to do a job by working for someone skilled at that job

**capitalism** an economic system in which owners run businesses for profit

**cholera** a disease spread by dirty water

**class** a system of organizing people according to their place in society, such as working class or middle class

**cliffhanger** an exciting end to a part of a story that leaves the audience in suspense

**colleagues** people someone works with

**commission** an instruction or request to do something for money

**congregate** to gather

**construction** building work

**contemporary** modern, of the present time

**debates** arguments about a topic

**debt** money owed

**debtor** a person who owes money

**democracy** a system of government in which all people in a country can vote

**disinherit** to prevent someone from acquiring property from their parents

**encounter** to meet up with someone without planning to

**engravings** pictures carved into a hard surface

**guardians** people who look after something

**heiress** a girl or woman who will inherit a lot of money

**incipient** beginning to happen or develop

**incredulity** amazement or disbelief

**industrial** related to industry

**Industrial Revolution** a period of rapid introduction of machines and steam power in the late 1700s and 1800s

**industrialists** people who are in favor of and involved in anything to do with industry

**industrialized** dominated by industry such as factories, mills, and mines

**inevitable** sure to happen

**influential** power to affect people

**inherit** to receive property from someone when they die

**installment** one part of a story that is published over time in a series of parts

**lectures** lessons or talks given to an audience

**legal system** system by which laws are made and carried out

**manufactured** made in a factory

**manure** animal waste

**material poverty** to have very few possessions

**menial** describes a job that requires little skill

**methodically** very carefully

**moral** related to right and wrong

**national debt** the total amount of money a government has borrowed

**nutritious** food that is full of nutrients, such as vitamins and minerals

**orphan** a child whose parents are dead

**pickpockets** thieves who steal from people's pockets

**plight** a difficult or unfortunate situation

**pneumonia** a dangerous illness that affects the lungs

**poverty** severe financial hardship

**profit** money made after all costs have been paid

**recognition** knowing something or recognizing something

**reform** a change that improves something

**relevant** meaningful

**rookeries** crowded slums associated with criminal activity

**salvation** to be saved

**sanitation** the provision of clean water and removal of sewage for public health

**satirical** making fun of something

**serial** a story that appears in installments

**slums** dirty, overcrowded residential districts in cities

**smog** fog mixed with smoke

**spectators** people who watch something, such as a public event

**squalor** the state of being very dirty and unpleasant

**steam engine** an engine powered by steam from water heated by fire

**topical** relevant to current events

**transforms** changes dramatically

**undertaker** a person who deals with dead bodies

**urban** related to towns or cities

**urbanization** the movement of people from the countryside to towns and cities

**villain** a bad person

# FOR MORE INFORMATION

## BOOKS

Dickens, Charles, adapted by Lisa Mullarkey. *Oliver Twist*. Edina, MN:
Magic Wagon, 2011.

Dickens, Charles. *The Charles Dickens Collection*. London, UK:
Arcturus, 2018.

Pollack, Pam. *Who Was Charles Dickens?* New York, NY:
Grosset & Dunlap, 2014.

Williams, Marcia. *Oliver Twist and Other Great Dickens Stories*.
London, UK: Walker Books, 2007.

## WEBSITES

Charles Dickens—www.charlesdickensinfo.com/life/timeline
This page features a timeline of the major events of Dickens's life.

Charles Dickens—
www.dkfindout.com/us/history/victorian-britain/charles-dickens/
This page includes a brief biography of Dickens's life.

*Oliver Twist* —www.charlesdickensinfo.com/novels/oliver-twist
This page has details about how Dickens wrote *Oliver Twist*.

# INDEX